THE

DAILY SPARK

180 easy-to-use lessons and class activities!

THE DAILY SPARK

Critical Thinking
Journal Writing
Poetry
Pre-Algebra
SAT: English Test Prep
Shakespeare
Spelling & Grammar
U.S. History
Vocabulary
Writing

THE
DAILY SPARK

Journal Writing

SPARKNOTES is a registered trademark of SparkNotes LLC.

Spark Publishing
A Division of Barnes & Noble
120 Fifth Avenue
New York, NY 10011
www.sparknotes.com

ISBN-13: 978-1-4114-0221-8
ISBN-10: 1-4114-0221-9

Please submit comments or report errors to www.sparknotes.com/errors.

Printed and bound in Canada.

Written by Christine Hood.

Introduction

The *Daily Spark* series gives teachers an easy way to transform downtime into productive time. The 180 exercises—one for each day of the school year—will take students five to ten minutes to complete and can be used at the beginning of class, in the few moments before turning to a new subject, or at the end of class.

The exercises in this book may be photocopied and handed out to the class, projected as a transparency, or even read aloud. In addition to class time use, they can be assigned as homework exercises or extra credit problems.

The *Journal Writing Daily Spark* shows students how fulfilling journal writing can be. It asks exciting, sometimes challenging questions about everything from school to scary dreams to siblings. It encourages students to analyze themselves and their lives, and it strives to get students in the habit of writing.

Spark your students' interest with the *Journal Writing Daily Spark*!

The Worst Time of Life

What was your most humiliating junior high experience? Write a short, possibly funny, description of it.

About My School

You have been chosen to describe your school in a brochure that will be given to students who live across the country. Assume that your readers know nothing about your city or school. Address the following topics:

Dialect/sayings
Dress
Mannerisms
Customs
Character types
Groups/cliques
Best thing
Worst thing
The one thing your readers should know

About My Name

Many names have special meaning or history. For example, the name Hannah means "favor" or "grace." The name Vito means "life."

Write about your own name. Who named you? What does your name mean? Does it have a special ethnic or religious significance? Are you named after someone in your family? If you could change your name, would you?

© 2004 SparkNotes LLC

Code of Chivalry

King Arthur of the Round Table is a heroic figure of English legend. Arthur and his knights were said to live by a set of beliefs known as the Code of Chivalry. A few rules of the code include:

- Live one's life so that it is worthy of respect and honor.
- Live for freedom, justice, and all that is good.
- Be polite and attentive.
- Never betray a confidence or a comrade.
- Protect the innocent.

Come up with a modern Code of Chivalry. Write a list of at least ten things people should do today to make modern society more chivalrous—that is, more considerate and courteous.

What I've Learned

Imagine you are moving to a foreign country and won't see your friends and family for many years. Write a letter to a friend or sibling, shelling out some words of wisdom and explaining how you would have done certain things differently.

Childhood Memories

Most people have vivid memories of certain events from childhood. What sticks in your mind? Pick one particularly strong memory and describe it in detail.

The Big Event

When a special event is on the horizon, people plan for it and get excited about it. Maybe it's a dance, an election, a family event, a party, a birthday, or an important sports game.

Think of a special event that you planned for and looked forward to that turned out much differently from what you expected. Write about what you expected would happen and what actually happened.

The Common Shakespeare

Shakespeare had an enormous working vocabulary; he used about 29,000 different words in his plays and poems. (By contrast, most people today have working vocabularies of only around 9,000 words.) Many people think of Shakespeare's language as difficult to understand, but he invented many words and phrases that we use nearly every day.

Below are some common phrases from Shakespearean plays. Choose one phrase, and explain what you think it means.

Apple of her eye
Eating me out of house and home
Good riddance
Green-eyed monster

All the world's a stage
To thine own self be true
Tower of strength
Wear my heart on my sleeve

© 2004 SparkNotes LLC

A Sense of Sports

People feel passionately about sports. Some play sports and detest it, because they're not as good as they want to be; others play and love it, because they're competitive and skilled. Some pay close attention to pro or local teams. Some attend games as serious fans; others attend because they like the social interaction in the stands. Some people loathe sports and think that the people who play them and watch them are brainless jocks. Which group do you fall into? Explain.

Musical Memories

A Sense of Sports

Songs can invoke vivid memories; hearing a particular song can rocket you back to seventh grade or last summer. Write about a song that is really evocative of a certain time in your life.

Alone at Last!

Your parents just left on a weeklong vacation—leaving you all alone, in charge of the house. What do you do? Instantly call your friends and announce a party? Decide to have a party and then regret it when you're cleaning for six hours the next day? Worry and don't do anything?

A Blooming Pear Tree

Read the following passage from Zora Neale Hurston's novel *Their Eyes Were Watching God*:

"Oh, to be a pear tree—any tree in bloom! With kissing bees singing of the beginning of the world! She was sixteen. She had glossy leaves and bursting buds and she wanted to struggle with life but it seemed to elude her. Where were the singing bees for her? . . . Looking, waiting, breathing short with impatience. Waiting for the world to be made."

Hurston compares the girl to a blooming pear tree, impatient and bursting with life. What metaphor from nature do you think best describes you? Write a short paragraph likening yourself to whatever animal, plant, landscape, or weather that most reminds you of yourself.

If I Could Meet . . .

If you could meet anyone, alive or dead, who would it be? Consider scientists, entertainers, world leaders, artists, writers, people in your family, and so on. Make a list of questions you'd like to ask this person.

Friend Types

Do you have one best friend? Are you the kind of person who goes everywhere in big groups? Or are you more of a loner? Write about the kind of "friend person" you are.

Remembering Firsts

There are many firsts in our lives that we don't remember, such as our first tooth, first step, first word, or first birthday. Firsts from later in childhood come easily to mind: a first pet, a first award, the first day of high school, a first kiss, a first summer at camp. Write about a special first that you remember clearly.

15

DAILY SPARK

JOURNAL WRITING

© 2004 SparkNotes LLC

To Be Great

Dr. Martin Luther King Jr. once said,

> **"Everyone has the power for greatness, not for fame, but greatness, because greatness is determined by service."**

Do you agree that everyone has the potential for greatness? Maybe you think serving others isn't what makes someone great; if that's the case, what do you think are the qualifying features of greatness?

If I Were in Charge

Most families set rules for their children, especially regarding behavior and responsibility. Which rules do you find particularly annoying? Do you long to stay out later, go out more, or dress any way you like? Write about the rules that you consider most unfair.

My Own Private Utopia

A **utopia**, according to *Webster's* dictionary, is "any place or state of ideal perfection." One person's utopia might be a country where discrimination does not exist and all lifestyles are tolerated. Another person's utopia might be a huge city full of clubs, theaters, and restaurants. What is your idea of utopia? If you could design the ideal society, what kind of laws would govern it? What would it look like? What kind of people would live there?

How Embarrassing!

Life is chock-full of embarrassing moments. When you're lying awake at night, having trouble sleeping, do your most embarrassing blunders run through your mind? Write about some of these agonizing memories.

© 2004 SparkNotes LLC

Dr. Seuss's Philosophy

In Dr. Seuss's *Horton Hears a Who,* Horton the elephant discovers a tiny planet of living beings on a speck of dust. Other animals urge Horton to throw away the dust speck, not believing that such a tiny world could exist, but Horton refuses. The book ends with this moral:

"A person is a person, no matter how small."

Write about a current political situation that you think illustrates the idea that even seemingly inconsequential people are important. Use Dr. Seuss's moral as the last sentence of your paragraph.

DAILY SPARK

JOURNAL WRITING

© 2004 SparkNotes LLC

The Center of the Earth

Imagine that you know nothing about science. As such a person, what do you think is at the center of the Earth? Come up with a few theories.

Other Life in the Universe

What is your opinion about the possibility of life on other planets? Do you need to see it to believe it, or do you believe that in a universe as vast as ours, alien life must exist? Write on the topic, beginning with the sentence,

I believe (don't believe) there is life on other planets because . . .

Overcoming Obstacles

Obstacles constantly present themselves. Some are fleeting, such as facing an important test in school. Some may take years to overcome, such as a major injury or the loss of a loved one. Write about an obstacle you've faced in your life. Did the experience change you for the better, or did it leave you bitter and cynical?

Like Hemingway

Read the following passage from Ernest Hemingway's novel *The Sun Also Rises*. In it, Hemingway conveys gloominess and dread by describing the weather.

"In the morning it was raining. A fog had come over the mountains from the sea. You could not see the tops of the mountains. The plateau was dull and gloomy, and the shapes of the trees and the houses were changed. I walked out beyond the town to look at the weather. The bad weather was coming over the mountains from the sea."

Write a passage that conveys a mood by describing the weather.

Holiday Cheer

What is your favorite holiday? What is your least favorite holiday? Write about two memorable holiday experiences, one from your favorite holiday and one from your least favorite.

Everyday Heroes

How do you define **hero**? Do you think fame is an important component of heroism, or do you think most heroes are unknown? Is there anyone you know personally whom you consider a hero?

Making a Comeback

According to the cliché,

"Every setback is an opportunity for a comeback."

In your life, has this proven true? Have you always recovered from setbacks?

Personal Personification

Personification is a literary device that gives a nonliving object the characteristics of a living thing. For example, a writer might say that the wind sighs, the rain laughs, and the leaves whisper. The poet Carl Sandburg wrote a poem called "Fog" that begins with personification:

"The fog comes on little cat feet."

Write a second line, rhymed or unrhymed, to follow Sandburg's line. For example:

The fog comes on little cat feet,
And creeps silently past my bedroom window.

If I Were President . . .

You have just been elected president of the United States of America. You must address foreign policy, terrorism, healthcare, the military, the economy, education, the environment, and much more. What are the first three things you will do? Which issues are dearest to your heart? Do you think those issues overlap with the issues that are most important to the American public?

Quirky Traditions

A **tradition** is a special ritual shared by a group of people. Families and groups of friends practice traditions throughout the year. These traditions might have to do with holidays, celebrations, food, the season, or quirky family practices that have been passed down from generation to generation. Is there a tradition that you share with your family or friends? Describe it.

My Animal

Which animal do you think you resemble most closely? Consider quiet, retiring animals like mice; bold and fearless ones like lions; eager, friendly ones like dogs; and finicky, secretive ones like cats. Consider your appearance, your personality, and the way you move. Then write about the animal with which you feel a kinship, explaining how you are similar in personality, characteristics, and/or physical features.

All Alone

Mark Twain once said,

"The worst loneliness is not to be comfortable with oneself."

What do you think he meant by this? Does this idea apply to your own life? Conclude your entry by explaining how you feel about being alone. Do you dread it, or do you enjoy having time to yourself?

JOURNAL WRITING

This I Believe

You probably share a basic outlook on life with your friends. However, most people have a few beliefs that would shock their friends. Write about a belief of yours that annoys or surprises the people who are close to you.

Treasure or Trash

To the naked eye it looks like junk, but you know it's precious: the beat-up stuffed animal you slept with every night as a kid, the raggedy baseball mitt you used in Little League, the tooth you couldn't bear to throw away after it fell out. Choose a beloved object from your own childhood, and explain why you feel sentimental about it or treasure it so much.

Types of Love

An almost infinite variety of types of love exists. The love of parents for their children is very different from the love of brothers for their sisters, of wives for their husbands, of kids for their pets, and on and on. Choose two people in your life whom you love, and explain how your love for each of them is different.

The Boob Tube

"Television hangs on the questionable theory that whatever happens anywhere should be sensed everywhere. If everyone is going to be able to see everything, in the long run all sights may lose whatever rarity value they once possessed, and it may well turn out that people, being able to see and hear practically everything, will be specially interested in almost nothing."

—E. B. White

You could argue that these days, everyone is able to see everything, particularly since Americans watch around four hours of TV per day. Do you think White's forecast was correct? Have extraordinary sights been cheapened by TV? Are people more scattered in their interests because of TV?

No Women Stand-ups

Despite huge advancements in recent years, women still struggle for respect in some fields. Many people still believe that women should not be allowed to pursue certain careers, especially those that are dangerous, require physical strength, or have traditionally been pursued by men. Many people are uncomfortable with the idea of a woman holding high political office; some people object to female stand-up comedians, claiming that most women aren't funny. Do you think women should be able to hold any kind of job they want, regardless of danger and tradition? Or do you believe that some jobs are only appropriate for men?

The Chicken or the Egg?

Which came first, violence in the media or a violent society? Some people believe that the casual violence in movies and TV desensitizes people, making them more violent. Others believe the exact opposite—that movies and television are simply a reflection of our society, which is becoming ever more violent on its own. What do you think?

Beauty or Brains?

"Beauty is only skin deep," the cliché claims. If you had to choose between beauty and brains, which would you pick? Which do you think would get you further in life? Which do you think would make you happier?

Cut Back

"Cut back on your possessions. The more you own, the more time you waste taking care of things."

—The Delany Sisters

As a brain-stretching exercise, it's useful to defend a position you don't actually agree with. Decide what you think about the recommendation above, and then argue the **opposite** position.

Must-See TV

Traditional sitcoms have been struggling to maintain their audiences, which are increasingly turning to reality TV. Suppose you've been asked to revitalize the sitcom industry by creating a new, original show. Write two paragraphs about your show, explaining what it's about, where it will be set, and what kind of actors it will star.

Oh Yeah? Oh Yeah?

You're never as witty and smart in the middle of a confrontation as you are after it's over, when suddenly you can think of a million things you should have said. Imagine you are back in the thick of an argument you once had, and write out the eloquent, intelligent remarks you should have made at the time.

Pick the Parent

Do you think you are more like your mother or more like your father? Or do you think you resemble one in looks, and the other in personality? Whom would you rather resemble?

Nature vs. Nurture

The "nature versus nurture" debate refers to the question of what influences us the most. Some scientists believe that nature (inherited genetic characteristics) shapes us as people. Others believe that nurture (our upbringing and other social influences) shapes us. What do you think? Do you think that genetics determine what we will become, or do the people and things around us have a greater influence?

New Beginnings

Maya Angelou was the first woman to read at a presidential inauguration. At the inauguration of President Bill Clinton in 1993, she read from her poem "On the Pulse of Morning." Below is an excerpt from the poem:

"History, despite its wrenching
    pain,
Cannot be unlived, and if faced
    with courage,
Need not be lived again.
Lift up your eyes upon

The day breaking for you.
Give birth again
To the dream.
Women, children, men . . .
Lift up your hearts.
Each new hour holds new chances"

What do you think this excerpt means? Do you consider the poem a suitable choice for an inauguration? Why or why not?

The Price of Technology

Technology has led to the discovery of vaccines and medical treatments. It has brought computers and televisions into people's homes, and it has provided us with electricity, the internet, phones, cars, planes, and much more. But an argument can be made that technology has largely worsened the quality of our lives, polluting the air, making our lives needlessly stressful, and dampening our enthusiasm for books.

If you had to give up one technological advantage that you use all the time, what would it be? Do you think you'd be better off without it?

The Perfect Friend

Some people might look for friends who are wild, aggressive, and daring; others might look for friends who are smart, funny, and loyal. List at least ten qualities you think the perfect friend should possess, ranked in order from most to least important. Do you know anyone who comes close to being the "perfect" friend?

Going Steady

Slang changes wildly from generation to generation, dating slang included. Kids of yore used to "get pinned"—a guy would literally give a pin to a girl he was dating in order to show that they were an item. What bizarre euphemisms have you heard adults use to describe dating? List a few and then write about how you respond when you hear adults use them.

Pot Shots

"Whenever you feel like criticizing anyone, just remember that all the people in this world haven't had the advantages you've had."

—F. Scott Fitzgerald

It's easy—and often really fun—to criticize people we don't know. Do you feel you're fair to other people, especially those you don't know very well, or do you criticize too much? Write about your tendency to be critical or fair.

Dear Famous Person . . .

Choose a famous historical figure you admire. This person could be a president, actor, athlete, scientist, author, artist, activist, humanitarian, or anyone else you find interesting. Write a letter to this person, explaining why you admire his or her accomplishments and how he or she has affected your life.

Cop, Doctor, Dancer

When you're a little kid, the professional world seems pretty appealing: firefighter, doctor, nurse, and astronaut are among the high-profile gigs you're aware of. As you get older, you realize that the mere desire to be an NBA star or a famous painter doesn't guarantee success. What was your ideal job when you were little? What do you imagine yourself doing now?

Wonderful Words

English, perhaps more than any other language, is full of descriptive, evocative words. For example, we don't just *walk*, we *amble, sashay, skip, lumber, tip-toe, stride, saunter, move, step, ramble,* or *stroll.* Some words (*luscious, dillydallying*) are fun to pronounce; others (*plop, slither*) sound like their meaning. What is your favorite word? What is your least favorite word? Explain your choices.

DAILY SPARK

JOURNAL WRITING

Offend Nobody

"If all printers were determined not to print anything till they were sure it would offend nobody, there would be very little ever printed."

—Benjamin Franklin

What do you think about censorship? Citizens of the United States are guaranteed the right to free speech, but many Americans feel that this right sometimes comes under attack. Have you seen evidence of this around you, even in your school? If not, have you read about anything that could be construed as censorship occurring in the United States?

The Nature Nut

Are you a nature fan, or would you sooner eat cockroaches than voluntarily go on a hike? Write about your best or worst nature experience.

Delivery

You answer a knock at the door and find a delivery guy holding a package for you. You open it up and find . . . what? Describe the best package you can imagine receiving.

Sibling Rivalry

Growing up with brothers and sisters can be difficult. If you have siblings, discuss the benefits and shortcomings of your situation. If you're an only child, do the same. Would you rather have more siblings, or fewer? Do you think you'll feel the same when you're middle-aged?

To Live Deliberately

DAILY SPARK

JOURNAL WRITING

"I went to the woods because I wished to live deliberately, to front only the essential facts of life, and see if I could not learn what it had to teach, and not, when I came to die, discover that I had not lived."

—Henry David Thoreau

What do you think Thoreau means by the phrase "to live deliberately"? Do you think you live deliberately?

Super Powers

Superheroes have it pretty good. Sure, a lot of them are lonely and misunderstood, but, as compensation, they can create massive storms at will, or fly, or shoot swords out of their fingers. If you could have any power, what would you choose, and why? What would you do with your new power?

Deserted Island

Suppose you will be stranded on a deserted island in the middle of the ocean for ten years. You will be allowed to bring one each of the following: book, movie, CD, food item, drink item, piece of clothing, and one miscellaneous item. List the one item you would bring in each category, and explain why you chose it.

Fly on the Wall

You know what you think about your friends, but what do they think about you? If you could eavesdrop on them talking about you, what do you think you would hear? Who would defend you? Who would criticize you most vigorously?

A Story of Food

In Laura Esquivel's novel *Like Water for Chocolate*, each chapter begins with a recipe that gradually turns into a narrative. For example, one chapter begins with instructions for preparing Christmas rolls:

"Take care to chop the onion fine. To keep from crying when you chop it (which is so annoying!), I suggest you place a little bit on your head. The trouble with crying over an onion is that once the chopping gets you started and the tears begin to well up, the next thing you know you just can't stop. I don't know whether that's ever happened to you, but I have to confess it's happened to me, many times. . . ."

Think of a food that provokes strong emotion in you, perhaps because it reminds you of your childhood or because you were eating it when something dramatic happened. Taking Esquivel's passage as a model, write the recipe for this food, and gradually shift into narrative, explaining why the food is meaningful to you. Include lots of descriptive, sensory adjectives.

The Official Parent Book

When you're young, it seems like your parents have some kind of official book called *How to Be an Adult* that tells them everything they need to know. At some point, you realize they're winging it just like everyone else; they don't really have all the answers. Do you remember a specific instance when you realized to your surprise that your parents were confused, scared, or irrational? How did you feel at that moment?

On My Headstone

An **epitaph** is a sometimes humorous saying or poem engraved on a headstone. For example:

Here lies the body of our Anna
Done to death by a banana;
It wasn't the fruit that laid her low
But the skin of the thing that made her go.

What epitaph would you want on your headstone? Would it be funny? Sweet? Serious? Write a draft of your epitaph.

It's Alive!

If you could bring one inanimate object to life, what would it be? Your mother's prom dress, your teacher's mirror, your boyfriend's or girlfriend's bedroom wall? What questions would you ask this object? Write your conversation in screenplay form.

I'm Nobody! Who Are You?

What follows is part of a poem by Emily Dickinson, an American poet.

I'M NOBODY! Who are you?
Are you—Nobody—Too?
Then there's a pair of us?
Don't tell! They'd advertise—
    you know!

How dreary—to be—Somebody!
How public—like a Frog—
To tell one's name—the livelong
    June—
To an admiring Bog!

Using this excerpt as a frame, write about who you are. (Don't worry about rhyming every line.)

I'M _____! Who are you?
Are you—_____—Too?
Then there's a pair of us?
Don't _____! They'd _____—you
    know!

How _____—to be—_____!
How _____—like a Frog—
To tell one's _____—the livelong
    _____—
To a (an) _____!

"Just So" Stories

Rudyard Kipling wrote a series of famous stories called *Just So Stories*. These stories create myths to explain how the leopard got its spots, how the rhinoceros got its skin, and how the camel got its hump. For example, Kipling imagines that the camel was lazy and said only "Humph!" whenever he was asked to work. Finally, as punishment, his "humph" turned into a hump. This way, the camel could work for three days straight without eating or drinking. Write your own Just So Story to explain how an animal came by a certain characteristic.

Good Luck Charms

Good luck charms range from stones to coins to horseshoes to plants (like a four-leaf clover) to certain animal parts (like a rabbit's foot). Some people carry personal objects that they consider lucky, such as a rubber band, picture, or letter. Do you have a good luck charm? Do you consider charms a silly fantasy? Do you carry one even though you're skeptical about its power?

Apples on Cheeks

Making big decisions is scary, and it's comforting to believe that you can rely on fate to make decisions for you. In the old days, a common courtship ritual practiced by women was to name several apple seeds after their suitors. The woman would put the moist seeds on her cheeks, and whichever seed stuck the longest told her which man she would marry. Do you think we've banished all such rituals from modern life, or do we still rely on them sometimes?

DAILY SPARK JOURNAL WRITING

© 2004 SparkNotes LLC

The Best Education

"The best education in the world is that got by struggling to get a living."

—Wendell Phillips

Many students sick of high school make arguments similar to Phillips's. Do you agree with Phillips that hard work provides a sufficient education, or do you think success is more likely for those people who receive a traditional education?

What a Fright

There's "fun scary" (walking through a haunted house, screaming through a horror movie, riding a roller coaster) and then there's "scary scary" (being in a car accident, getting caught in the ocean's riptide). Describe the scariest experience you've ever had. Was it fun scary, or was it really terrifying?

The Best Year

Is there one year of your life that stands out as exceptional? Maybe you starred in a play, or you suddenly became very popular, or your mother was in a yearlong fantastic mood. Describe this year.

Hit the Jackpot

Suppose you win $10 million in the lottery, but there's a catch: You have to donate half of the money to charity. What charity would you choose? What would you do with the money you got to keep?

Literature for Life

"What we call education and culture is for the most part nothing but the substitution of reading for experience, of literature for life, of the obsolete fictitious for the contemporary real."

—George Bernard Shaw

Someone who hates reading could use Shaw's words to argue that books merely distract from real life. Whatever your feelings on the matter, write a rebuttal to the anti-reader, explaining why literature is an important part of life.

No TV

74

DAILY SPARK

JOURNAL WRITING

Before the age of television, people entertained themselves largely by reading, telling stories, playing music, chatting, and doing things outside. If you had to stop watching TV for one month, how would you fill your time? Would you miss TV terribly, or would you welcome the break?

Miss/Mr. Manners

DAILY SPARK

JOURNAL WRITING

© 2004 SparkNotes LLC

Good manners, we're always told, are of crucial importance. But the definition of good manners shifts with the passage of time. Years ago, children were expected to call their elders (sometimes even their parents) "sir" and "ma'am." This practice has largely been dropped in the United States. What modern component of good manners do you think will seem bizarre and old-fashioned in fifty years?

A Star Is Born

If you were allowed to star in the movie of your choice, what kind of movie would you choose? Pick out your costars, your shooting location, and your wardrobe. Include, if you like, your action sequences and the martial arts you'd learn.

The Road Ahead

"Each of us has the right and the responsibility to assess the road which lies ahead and those over which we have traveled, and if the feature road looms ominous or unpromising, and the road back uninviting, then we need to gather our resolve and carrying only the necessary baggage, step off that road into another direction. If the new choice is also unpalatable, without embarrassment, we must be ready to change that one as well."

—Maya Angelou

What is Angelou saying about courage and decisions? Do you think this is a helpful way to look at life? Talk about a time in your own life when you had to change courses.

We Present You With . . .

Consider the bevy of awards available to the world's high achievers: the Nobel Peace Prize for contributing to world peace, the Webby for web design, the Clio for advertising, the Oscar for the film industry, the Tony for theater, the Emmy for television, the Pulitzer Prize for writing, the Grammy for music, the Cy Young for pitching—the list goes on and on. If you could be presented with one of these prestigious awards, which one would you choose? Describe the specific accomplishment that would win you the award.

DAILY SPARK

JOURNAL WRITING

© 2004 SparkNotes LLC

Five Senses, Minus One

Most people are born with five senses—sight, hearing, touch, taste, and smell. If you had to give up one sense for the rest of your life, which would you pick, and why?

Love at First Sight

Literature and film are full of characters who fall in love at first sight. Do you believe this kind of love is possible? Do you believe two people can look at each other and fall instantly in love, knowing they are meant to be together? Has this ever happened to you? Explain how you feel about this idealistic notion.

Starry Night

In the following passage from Shakespeare's *Romeo and Juliet*, the character Juliet talks to the night as she waits for Romeo to come to her:

"Come, gentle night; come, loving, black-browed night,
Give me my Romeo: and, when he shall die,
Take him and cut him out in little stars,
And he will make the face of heaven so fine,
That all the world will be in love with night,
And pay no worship to the garish sun."

Imagine that you're waiting for the love of your life, and write a short poem or paragraph addressed to whatever you're looking at as you wait.

A Dream Come True

It's sometimes incredibly boring to listen to other people talk about their dreams, but always incredibly fun to talk at length about your own. Well, now's your chance: Describe your most terrifying nightmare, your recurring dream, and the dream you wish had been real.

You Make the Law

You have been called to Washington, D.C. For some inexplicable reason, the president wants you to add an amendment of your choosing to the Constitution. What would you add? Write out your new amendment, and explain how you hope it will affect or help the people of the United States.

Masculine and Feminine

People have different ideas about what is masculine and what is feminine behavior. List five attributes or activities that you consider feminine and five attributes or activities that you consider masculine. Do you think your list is pretty typical, or do you think it would anger a lot of people? Explain your answer.

Exemption from Prejudice

"There is no prejudice so strong as that which arises from a fancied exemption from all prejudice."

—William Hazlitt

Hazlitt suggests that those people who are most convinced they're not prejudiced are actually most vulnerable to holding prejudices. Do you think he's right? Do you know anyone who proves him right? Discuss your thoughts on the matter.

Tiny or Immense

Decisions, decisions. They range from the tiny (*Should I have tuna or turkey for lunch?*) to the immense (*Should I accept that scholarship or follow my dreams and become a cowboy?*). If you could go back in time and change one decision you've made, what would it be? Why do you regret making this decision?

Secret Camera

Suppose you've been given an invisible camera. You can put it anywhere in the world—the Oval Office, the teacher's lounge, a movie star's apartment—and watch what happens. Where would you put such a camera?

I'm Sorry

Apologizing is hard to do. Sometimes you can't bring yourself to do it, or sometimes your attempt to apologize just infuriates the other person even more. Write about an apology you wish you'd made or an apology that went awry when you tried to make it.

DAILY SPARK JOURNAL WRITING

© 2004 SparkNotes LLC

Ode to Object

Poets in the romantic movement wrote about nature in inspired, sometimes melodramatic tones. Think of an element in nature—something very simple, like a twig, a blade of grass, or a ladybug. Then write an ode of praise to this object, portraying it as extraordinary and important.

15 Minutes

Ode to Object

Pop artist Andy Warhol once said that in the future, every person will experience fifteen minutes of fame in his or her lifetime. The advent of reality TV, among other phenomena, has certainly made many average people briefly famous. What do you think would make you famous for fifteen minutes? Consider your own skills, ambition, and geographic location.

The Perfect Day

Describe a perfect day—not the one you'd have if you were rich and famous, but the one you could have this Saturday or Tuesday. What day of the week would your perfect day fall on? What would you do, see, eat, read, watch?

Dare to Date

Say you've met an amazing person you're dying to date. This person feels the same way about you. The problem is that this person has a quality your family would flip out about, even though you don't think it's a big deal. Maybe it's this person's age, race, occupation, religion, or interests. What about a potential boyfriend or girlfriend would drive your parents insane? Do you think you'd back down and not date this person if your family made a huge fuss, or would you stick to your guns?

Making a Life

"An educational system isn't worth a great deal if it teaches young people how to make a living but doesn't teach them how to make a life."

—Anonymous

React to this quotation by reflecting on how it applies to you and your future. Do you feel your education has taught you how to make a living and how to make a life? Will you rely on college to teach you about life, or do you feel your current level of education is sufficient?

Spilled Popcorn

What's the worst movie you've seen recently? Imagine you're a film critic and write a couple of paragraphs tearing this movie to shreds.

© 2004 SparkNotes LLC

DAILY SPARK

JOURNAL WRITING

© 2004 SparkNotes LLC

Generation Representation

For many people, the passage of time reduces history to a series of oversimplified images and ideas. We associate the 1950s with prosperity and conservatism; the 1960s with social upheaval, experimentation, and war; the 1970s with self-examination; the 1980s with prosperity and decadence. How do you think history will reduce the events of your generation? What will people associate with your generation in the future?

Generation Gap

Parents and children often claim to be misunderstood by each other. Explain one thing you think your parents (or other people their age) don't understand about your generation. Then explain one thing you think your parents would say your generation doesn't understand about them.

Prisoner of Prejudice

"Everyone is a prisoner of his own experiences. No one can eliminate prejudices—just recognize them."

—Edward R. Murrow

Murrow was a journalist and broadcaster. Do you think most journalists have prejudices? If so, do you think they recognize them? Do you think journalists' profession gives them a special obligation to examine themselves honestly?

I'm Grateful

Even the dreariest, most awful weeks aren't bad twenty-four hours a day. Think of a few things that have happened this week that you're grateful for.

Breaking Up

Woody Allen once said,

"It's better to be the leaver than the leavee."

Do you agree? Would you rather dump someone than get dumped yourself? Which do you think is more painful?

Identical Twin

Do you think it would be cool to have an identical twin? Sharing a birthday might get annoying, but the number of tricks you could pull off is practically infinite. If you had an identical twin, what prank would you pull first?

Kids in the Shade

"One generation plants the trees; another gets the shade."

—Chinese proverb

This proverb, which uses a simple metaphor to express a big idea, applies to all generations. Write about how you think this proverb relates to a current political situation in the United States.

Wanted: Great Employee

Write an ad pitching yourself to the employer of your choice. Think about what your employer might be looking for in an employee, and portray your strengths in the best possible light. Attempt to use catchy phrases and clever writing to advertise yourself.

Class Design

If you and your friends could choose one new class to add to the curriculum, what would it be? Think of what would most help you in your daily life or what would prepare you for life after graduation. What kind of assignments would be required, and how would the class benefit students?

Silly Superstitions

Spill the salt? Break a mirror? Let a black cat cross your path? Open an umbrella inside? Do these things and terrible bad luck will ensue, according to many people. Sometimes, even if people scoff at superstition, they'll still avoid walking under ladders . . . just in case. What's your position on the matter? Are you a superstitious person?

From Passive to Active

"We have not passed that subtle line between childhood and adulthood until we move from the passive voice to the active voice—that is, until we have stopped saying 'It got lost,' and say, 'I lost it.'"

—Sidney J. Harris

Harris uses grammar to make a larger point: that only when we start taking responsibility for our actions can we call ourselves adults. Write about a moment when you were tempted to use the passive voice (that is, to refuse to take responsibility) but ultimately decided to use the active voice.

Never Ever

Think about all of the older people you know—teachers, parents, coaches, neighbors, friends, relatives, acquaintances. Probably one or several of the adults you know have provided you with an example of how *not* to live your life. Look ahead to your future, and think about the one thing you will not let happen. Begin by writing: **The one thing I will never do is . . .**

Prom Night

Like it or not, you have to plan the prom. This involves finding a place to hold the dance, booking a band or a DJ, deciding on a theme, picking out the decorations, ordering food and drinks, and choosing chaperones. You have total control. What decisions would you make?

Boys and Girls

Do you think men or women have an easier time of things? Explain your thoughts.

Mother/Father

Use the following frame to write a poem about one of your parents:

When I was little, my mother/father (*describe two characteristics of your parent*)

I remember (*describe a memory of a day with your parent*)

That day, she/he (*describe something you remember this parent doing*)

It infuriated me when (*describe something about your parent that made you angry*)

When I was a child, life was (*mention two things about the quality of your life then*)

Now, my mother/father (*describe something that has changed since your childhood*)

Time Traveler

If you could go anywhere in the world, at any time in the past or future, where and to what time would you go? What would you want to see, and whom would you want to meet? Explain.

Choosing Genes

The genes you received from your mother and father have influenced the way you look and probably some characteristics of your personality. If you could choose which characteristics to receive from each parent, which ones would you pick? Choose and describe three characteristics from each parent, and explain why you want them.

Boys to Men/Girls to Women

Aside from physical considerations, what do you think is the main thing that differentiates a girl from a woman? A boy from a man?

Darkness and Light

"Darkness cannot drive out darkness; only light can do that. Hate cannot drive out hate; only love can do that."

—Dr. Martin Luther King Jr.

Dr. King was a pacifist and believed that hatred and prejudice could be fought with love. Do you agree with him? Do you think that in all situations a peaceful response is the correct one?

Keeping Secrets

When you confide in a friend, you hope he or she will keep your secret. Do you think there are some secrets you should not keep for a friend? Or do you think that it's always better to keep your promise and tell no one about your friend's secret, even if someone's in danger?

My Charity

Your state governor has contacted you directly about forming a new charity. You will be given all the funds you need to get started. You can form any charity you wish, to support any cause you deem worthy. Which cause would you support? Is there someone or something in particular that influenced your decision?

Dinner Party

If you could invite any three people from any period in history to a dinner party, whom would you invite? Describe each person, and explain why you chose him or her.

Love Is the Flower

"Love is the flower of life, and blossoms unexpectedly and without law, and must be plucked where it is found, and enjoyed for the brief hour of its duration."

—D. H. Lawrence

What is the first thing that comes to mind after reading this quotation? How does it make you feel? Whom or what does it make you think about?

Life Lessons

Based on what you've learned in your life so far, what two lessons do you think will be most important to teach your children? Are these two lessons also ones your parents have taught you, or do they come entirely from your own life and experiences?

In the Attic

You're staying with your grandparents. One day you venture up into the attic. Among all the cobwebs, old clothes, and dusty boxes you find a big old trunk. Curious, you open the lid . . . .

What would you like to find in that trunk (besides money)? Would you want to find something of monetary value? Would you want to find the old journals of a distant relative?

The Ideal Mate

Marriage is probably years and years away for you, but you might already have a vague idea of what you'll look for in an ideal mate. What do you imagine this person looks like? What kind of job will he or she have? Will he or she have to share your values and religious beliefs, or can you imagine being with someone quite different from you?

Whom Would You Call?

"If you were going to die soon and had only one phone call you could make, who would you call and what would you say? And why are you waiting?"

—Stephen Levine

Answer Levine's questions as openly and honestly as you can.

DAILY SPARK

JOURNAL WRITING

© 2004 SparkNotes LLC

Happiness

Whom Would You Call?

Some people think that we can be as happy as we decide to be. Others believe that events and circumstances beyond our control determine how happy we will be. Still others think that there are happy people who effortlessly maintain their sunny outlook no matter what happens, and unhappy people who usually feel depressed no matter what happens. What do you think? Is happiness something you can work at, or is it beyond your control?

Time Capsule

You are putting together a time capsule that will be buried in your backyard for 500 years. The capsule is about the size of a large suitcase. What would you put inside the capsule? What would you want future generations to know about today's world? What items best represent who you are? What items best represent your place in history?

Gender Gap

Misunderstandings and clichés about men and women persist, aided by such books as *Men Are from Mars, Women Are from Venus.* If you could forever banish one stereotype about your gender, which one would you choose? Why is this stereotype so annoying to you?

What Is Love, Anyway?

"People love others not for who they are, but for how they make them feel."

—Irwin Federman

In your experience, have you found Federman's statement to be true?

Mirror Image

When you look in the mirror, what do you see? Do you like what you see? What, if anything, would you change? Do you think others see you as you see yourself?

Under Pressure

Do you think your friends or your parents have a bigger influence on you? Has this changed as you've gotten older? Is there any issue that you feel strongly about, so strongly that neither your friends nor your family could influence you?

Five Years from Now

Imagine that you can see five years into the future. What is your life like, personally and professionally? Where are you living? Who are you with? What have you have accomplished?

Different Drummer

"Why should we be in such desperate haste to succeed, and in such desperate enterprises? If a man does not keep pace with his companions, perhaps it is because he hears a different drummer. Let him step to the music that he hears, however measured or far away."

—Henry David Thoreau

Thoreau urges us to follow our instincts rather than mindlessly rushing to compete with our peers. Do you know someone (possibly yourself) who marches to the beat of a different drummer? How does this person live differently from others? Do other people consider this person weird or misguided?

Two Lives

When an agonizing decision presents itself, it seems unfair that you can't somehow take two paths at once: take the great job and move to France; date this person and that person. Have you ever been in a tricky situation like this? Which of two tempting paths did you choose? Did you make the right decision?

DAILY SPARK

JOURNAL WRITING

© 2004 SparkNotes LLC

Truth or Fiction?

Do you believe you're generally an honest person? Do you find yourself telling people what you think they want to hear? Are you willing to tell a little lie if you need to make an excuse? Or are you the opposite—are you really blunt? Do you tell the truth even if you know it's going to annoy people?

First Impressions

Imagine you're alone with someone you've had a crush on for a while. What do you do and say to impress this person? If you could only tell this person two things about yourself, what would those two things be? What would you want this person to know about you that would make a good impression?

Holding Out Hope

"Reserving judgment is a matter of infinite hope."

—F. Scott Fitzgerald

Do you think people who refuse to think badly of other people are fools or optimists? Do you tend to make snap judgments about people? If so, is your initial impression usually right or wrong?

Taking the Blame

Have you ever taken the blame for something you didn't do? What were you blamed for, and why did you accept the responsibility? Were you protecting someone, or did you protest your innocence only to be met with disbelief? Describe the situation.

Ten Years after High School

Do you think you'll attend your high school reunion? Maybe you think it will be fun to see how everyone's doing; maybe you can't stand the people at your high school and can't wait to see the last of them; maybe you don't know what you'll feel in ten years. What do you think?

School Cliques

Are cliques a major part of your school? Are the popular kids a big, annoying presence? Are you one of those popular kids? Do you think cliques are an unavoidable part of school, or do you think they're preventable?

Like a Giant

In Shakespeare's *Measure for Measure*, the character Isabella tells the powerful duke,

> "O, it is excellent to have a giant's strength; but it is tyrannous to use it like a giant ."

Rewrite this statement in your own words, and then explain how it applies to a situation in your own life.

Standing Up

You just saw some upperclassmen picking on a freshman, who was crying. You're kind of friends with these upperclassmen, but you're not totally comfortable with them. Do you intervene or just walk away? Why?

JOURNAL WRITING

© 2004 SparkNotes LLC

That Was Then, This Is Now

Choose one of these topics to write about, fill in the blanks accordingly, and then write a paragraph about how you feel now:

School
My family
Romance
Prejudice

"When I was young, I thought that _____ was (were) _____, but now that I'm older, I see that . . ."

That Was Then, This Is Now II

Choose one of these topics to write about, fill in the blanks accordingly, and then write a paragraph about how you feel now:

Boyfriends/girlfriends
Friends
Summer
College
The future

"When I was young, I thought that _____ was (were) _____, but now that I'm older, I see that . . ."

He's Always on My Mind

"I *am* Heathcliff. . . . He's always on my mind—not as a pleasure, any more than I am always a pleasure to myself—but as my own being. . . ."

— Emily Brontë

People in love often proclaim that they are one with their boyfriend or girlfriend or that they think about their beloved all the time. Have you felt this way, or known friends who have? Do you think this feeling can be sustained, or is it just the excitement of a new relationship?

Morning Routine

"I raised my weary head from the white and fluffy cloud upon which it had rested. Ah, to face another day! My raven hair was strewn about my creased face like the wild feathers of a frightened bird."

This is the very melodramatic beginning of a description of a morning routine. In a similarly melodramatic tone, describe your morning routine.

Our Own Dictionary

You have been hired to write a dictionary of common terms, phrases, and slang used by you and your friends. Brainstorm a few entries.

If I Were Ahab

You've probably read books from a wide variety of **genres**—fairy tales, science fiction, poems, plays, romance, mysteries. If you could live the life of any character in fiction, whom would you choose, and why?

The Root of All Evil

You're probably heard the cliché "Money is the root of all evil ." Do you agree that the desire for money and the possession of money lead to corruption and violence, or do you think something else is the root of all evil?

Leader or Follower?

Are you a trendsetter? Do you take the lead in class or with your friends? Do your friends look to you to make decisions about what you're doing or where you're going? Or do you participate in groups without leading them? Do you go along with the things your friends decide? Are you comfortable with whichever role you play? Give a few examples.

DAILY SPARK · JOURNAL WRITING

Of Age

You have to reach a certain age to do many things, such as drive, drink, and vote. Do you agree with the legal ages in your state? If you think any of the laws should be changed, explain why.

Stargazing

Have you ever sat outside at night under a sky filled with twinkling stars? What do you think about when you look at the stars? Do you feel small in comparison to the universe above you, or is your focus on something else altogether? Describe your thoughts under a starry night sky.

The Art of Courtly Love

During the Middle Ages, "courtly love" was considered the highest form of love. According to the principles of courtly love, jealous people can't love; boys don't love until they reach the age of maturity; easily attained love doesn't have as much value as hard-to-attain love; and lovers always turn pale in the presence of their beloved.

Do any of these principles still apply, or do they seem hopelessly out of date? If you could write your own principles of love, what would they be?

The Mother of All Surprises

Write about a time when your parents really surprised you. Did this event or situation seem out of character for your parents? Was the surprise a good one or a bad one? What was your reaction?

Just by Looking

Do you think you can tell a lot about someone just by his or her appearance? Can you tell if someone is friendly or intelligent? Can you tell if the person has similar interests to you? Can you tell if the person is rich or poor?

Stranded

You went hiking with some friends, took off on your own for a while, and got lost. You've wandered around all day looking for your friends, but you can't find them anywhere. What is the first thing you do? Have you brought food, water, and maps along, or are you the freewheeling type who just comes as you are? What thoughts are going through your head? How do you feel? Write about the situation.

Famous Firsts of the 1900s

Read this list of famous firsts:

1903—Marie Curie becomes the first woman to win the Nobel Prize.

1932—Amelia Earhart becomes the first woman to make a transatlantic solo flight.

1945—Jackie Robinson becomes the first African-American baseball player to sign a formal contract in the major leagues.

1967—Thurgood Marshall becomes the first African-American Supreme Court justice.

1969—Neil Armstrong becomes the first man to walk on the moon.

1981—Sandra Day O'Connor becomes the first woman to become a U.S. Supreme Court justice.

Which one of these people would you most like to have been, and why?

I Wish You Knew

Is there something you wish your parents knew about you? Is there something you would confess to them if you could? How would you tell them? Do you think you would feel better if they knew?

Bad Habits

Bad habits range from nail-biting to overeating to procrastinating to gossiping. What are your bad habits? What can you live with, and what would you rather stamp out altogether?

155

DAILY SPARK

JOURNAL WRITING

© 2004 SparkNotes LLC

Senior Superlatives

The yearbook just came out, and you leaf through the pages eagerly. The superlative section lists the students who stood out in a variety of areas. The categories include "most talented," "most athletic," "best smile," "best sense of humor," "most unique," and "most likely to succeed." Which superlative would you most like to win? Why?

Money Matters

You probably spend your money (or your parents' money) on school supplies, food, clothes, movies, and gifts. Of all the things you've spent money on this year, what is the best spending decision you've made? What is the worst?

Platitudes or Shockers

Your school has selected you to give the final speech at high school graduation. What would you like to say to your fellow students? Would you confine yourself to platitudes and hopeful words, or would you rather shock your listeners with an angry or controversial speech?

Taking On the World

What do you think are the three most pressing problems facing the United States today? Do you have any ideas about how these problems might be solved? Do you think they will be solved in your lifetime?

(Un)lucky Me

Taking Out the World

Do you think you're generally a lucky or an unlucky person? Think about your quality of life, your health, your family, the frequency with which you win contests, and so on.

The Business of Choice

If you could own the business of your dreams, what would it be? Would it be a small business or a large business? What service or product would you sell? Where would it be located? Would you employ your friends?

A Mouse Click Away

Internet dating has become a popular and acceptable way to meet people. What do you think about the phenomenon? Do you think it's a good way to meet people? Do you think it's safe? Do you know anyone who has done it? Do you think you would do it yourself?

Looking Forward

What are you looking forward to this week, this month, this summer? What are you looking forward to doing once you turn eighteen? Once you graduate from high school? Write about what you're looking forward to in the short term and in the long term.

Explain to the Aliens

If you were trying to explain high school students to visiting aliens, how would you do it? Imagine that the aliens wanted you to classify teenagers into four groups. Consider personality, geographic location, race, class, intelligence, physical aptitude, and other factors, and then come up with your four groups.

DAILY SPARK

JOURNAL WRITING

Best Time, Right?

Some adult (or several adults) have probably told you, "This is the best time of your life, and you don't even know it ."

Do you have a sense that this is true, or do you think these adults are crazy? Can you imagine looking back on this period in your life in fifteen years and thinking that you didn't appreciate it enough, or are you convinced that you'll be happier later than you are now?

Why I'm Famous

If you could be famous for anything, what would you be famous for? You could be an inventor, an athlete with tons of championships and endorsement deals, a Pulitzer Prize–winning author, the scientist who discovers the cure for cancer, an Oscar-winning actor, a groupie-attracting rock star, or something else entirely.

DAILY SPARK JOURNAL WRITING

My Bedroom

Is your bedroom messy or tidy? How is it decorated? What kind of CDs and posters and books do you have? What is your furniture like? If someone who didn't know you walked into your bedroom, what do you think they would infer about you from what they see?

Full or Empty?

If someone always sees the glass as half empty, he is a pessimist—he sees that some of the drink is gone, whereas an optimist would focus on what remains. Do you consider yourself an **optimist** or a **pessimist**? Do you tend to focus on the negative or the positive? Give a few examples.

One Thing

If you had the power to change one thing about your school, what would it be, and why would you want to change it?

Three Virtues

Confucianism, which is practiced by approximately six million people around the world, is a life philosophy. It teaches its practitioners to live their lives according the universal virtues—wisdom, benevolence, and fortitude. If you were to develop your own life philosophy, what three things would you designate as your universal virtues?

Arranged Marriage

In some cultures, marriages are arranged. The parents, sometimes with the aid of a matchmaker, choose mates for their children. If your parents had to choose a mate for you, what kind of characteristics and qualities do you think they would look for? How would your parents' choices differ from your own?

Quiet Time

Most people need time to be alone, even if it's only once in a while. Do you go to a particular place when you want to be alone? Describe this place in detail. What about this place makes you feel relaxed? If you don't have a special place to be alone, describe one you would like to have.

The Year 3060

What do you think the world will be like in the year 2060? What kinds of cars, houses, and appliances will be available? Do you think people will be living on other planets? Do you think the world will be peaceful and harmonious?

Masters of Our Fate

In Shakespeare's *Julius Caesar*, the character Cassius tries to convince Brutus to overthrow Caesar, the leader of Rome. He tells Brutus,

"Men at some time are masters of their fates: The fault, dear Brutus, is not in our stars, but in ourselves, that we are underlings."

Do you believe in fate, or do you think people have complete power over their lives? Has any event in your own life convinced you that fate exists, or made you skeptical about it?

Introvert or Extrovert?

Do you think of yourself as an **extrovert**, someone who feels at ease around new people and enjoys being in groups? Or are you more of an **introvert**, someone who keeps to himself or herself and feels shy in large groups? Give some examples that show what kind of person you are.

Lyrical Lines

What is your favorite song? How do the words make you feel? What images or thoughts come to mind when you listen to it? Is this song currently popular, or is it a song from your childhood?

Compliments

Some people enjoy getting compliments and don't feel embarrassed by them. Others are uncomfortable hearing praise. Which kind of person are you? What types of compliments have you received? How did you feel about receiving these compliments? Were you embarrassed? Do you feel the person praising you was being honest? Did you feel more confident after hearing this praise? Explain your feelings.

Dogs and Cats

Do you prefer dogs or cats? Would you rather be around dogs, which tend to be loving and loyal, or cats, which tend to be independent? Explain your preference.

JOURNAL WRITING

When You Can't Brush

When you're a little kid, certain aspect of personal hygiene seem ridiculous (*Shower every day? Why, whatever for?*). What do you do religiously now that you found absurd when you were little?

You're Almost There

Looking forward to the end of the year? Yeah, thought so. What are you up to this summer? What would you do if you had all the money in the world and could go anywhere?